2

Mr. Lincoln's Whiskers

Mr. Lincoln's Whiskers

By Burke Davis

Illustrated by Douglas Gorsline

Coward, McCann & Geoghegan, Inc. • New York

Text copyright © 1978 by Burke Davis
Illustrations copyright © 1978 by Douglas Gorsline
All rights reserved. This book, or parts thereof, may
not be reproduced in any form without permission in
writing from the publisher. Published simultaneously
in Canada by Longman Canada Limited, Toronto.

Library of Congress Cataloging in Publication Data
Davis, Burke   Mr. Lincoln's whiskers.
Summary: At the suggestion of a young girl,
Abraham Lincoln grows a beard.
[1. Lincoln, Abraham, Pres. U. S., 1809-1865—
Fiction] I. Gorsline, Douglas W.   II. Title.
PZ7.D28556Mi   ISBN 0-698-20455-7   [Fic]   77-29208

Printed in the United States of America

Typography by Jane Breskin Zalben

To Elsie

One October morning in the year 1860 Abraham Lincoln rose early, as he usually did, and shaved himself. Outside his plain white-painted house, dawn was breaking over the small town of Springfield, Illinois.

While his wife slept, Mr. Lincoln lighted an oil lamp on his bedroom dresser and poured water from a pitcher into his shaving mug.

He smiled at the sight of his sleeping wife, who was now plump and middle-aged. He remembered her as the prettiest girl in Springfield, who had said even during her childhood that she was going to marry a President of the United States when she grew up.

Lincoln sharpened his razor on a leather strop and brushed soap lather over his long face. He peered into a mirror and guided the blade across the hollows of his cheeks.

With his left hand he smoothed the wrinkles from his loose brown skin and drew the razor carefully around a mole.

Mr. Lincoln was a modest man who liked to make jokes about himself. He smiled at his face in the mirror and his gray eyes crinkled beneath heavy brows. He ran a hand through his bristly black hair. "I must be the ugliest man in the world," he thought.

He grinned more widely when he remembered that his wife agreed with him. She often teased Mr. Lincoln. She had seen newspaper pictures of the men running for President, frowned at the one of her husband among those of more handsome men, and said half seriously, "A look at that face is enough to put an end to hope."

He remembered the night when he had met his wife, years before, at a dance. Someone had led the awkward Lincoln to the short, pretty Mary Todd and said, "Here's a man who wants to dance with you in the worst way." They danced for only a few minutes before Mary excused herself and sat down.

"Well, Mary," said a friend, "did he dance with you in the worst way?"

"Yes—the very worst."

Lincoln often told a story—which he pretended was true —of meeting an old woman on horseback as he was riding in the woods. The woman stared. "I do believe you are the ugliest man I ever saw," she said. "You're probably right," Lincoln said, "but I can't help it."

Lincoln always roared with laughter as he repeated the woman's last words. "No," she said. "You can't help it, but you might stay home."

Most Americans had seen Lincoln's face only in pictures, if at all, for though he was a well-known debater, he was not yet famous. He was still only a Springfield lawyer who spent most of his time in Illinois.

Not long before, Lincoln had run for a seat in the United States Senate and lost. He had taken his defeat with a smile. He had told a friend, "I feel like the boy who stubbed his toe —it hurt too much to laugh, and he was too big to cry."

Lincoln was now running for President as the candidate

of the new Republican Party, and Election Day was little

more than two weeks away. This was to be one of the most important elections in American history. People of the Southern states, who feared that Lincoln would put an end to black slavery, said those states would leave the Union—the United States—if he became President.

Southerners especially talked about how ugly Lincoln was. Newspaper cartoons in the South often showed him as a long-armed baboon.

Men who owned slaves remembered that Lincoln had said the nation could not live as a divided house—half slave and half free. The South would vote for Democrats who would help keep black slaves at work in fields of cotton, tobacco, and sugar cane.

Mr. Lincoln said he understood the feelings of the slaveholders perfectly. "It reminds me," he said, "of what an old boyhood friend once said about skinning eels: 'It don't hurt them so very much. It's been going on for such a long time, they're used to it.' "

On this October morning in 1860, at any rate, no one could be sure that the Republicans would win the election. Especially Mr. Lincoln.

"My trouble," Lincoln thought as he shaved, "is that I don't look like a President." His ears were too big. His

Gorsline

neck was too long. His large Adam's apple waggled when he spoke. He also looked old. People had begun calling him "Old Abe" when he was only thirty years old.

As he washed and dried his face that morning, Mr. Lincoln had no idea that he had shaved his long jaws for just about the last time in his life.

When he had dressed, Mr. Lincoln left his house and walked a block or so to a grocery store, where he bought a dime's worth of meat for his family's breakfast. He stalked along on a pair of legs that must have been some of the longest in the country. He was six feet four inches tall, weighed 180 pounds, and was like a scarecrow with his stooped shoulders and his black clothes hanging loosely on him. His coat and trousers were baggy, and not always brushed and clean. His big feet fell flat on the ground when he walked, and not heel first as most people walk.

Lincoln never seemed to mind when people teased him about his long legs. Once, when two men asked Lincoln to settle an argument about how long a man's legs should be in proportion to his body, he replied: "After much thought and consideration, not to mention mental worry and anxiety, it is my opinion that a man's lower limbs, in order to preserve harmony of proportion, should be at least long enough to reach from his body to the ground."

Lincoln usually wore a tall, black "stovepipe" hat, in which he kept many papers and letters—and sometimes, when he raised his hat to a lady on the street, his papers showered all about him.

One day when Lincoln left his tall hat on an office chair, a large woman came in and sat on the hat. When she arose, Lincoln smiled and said, "Madam, I could have told you it wouldn't have fitted."

Some of Lincoln's neighbors laughed at the idea of his becoming President, for to them he was plain Old Abe, who was not a rich man, and who refused to take himself very seriously.

Many people in Springfield agreed with an elderly Democrat who met Old Abe soon after his nomination and said, "So you're Abe Lincoln."

"Yes, that's my name."

"They say you're a self-made man."

"Well, yes. What there is of me is self-made."

The old man looked up and down Lincoln's gangling frame. "Well," he said, "all I've got to say is that it was a darned bad job."

This was another of Lincoln's favorite stories about himself, one that he told while shaking with laughter.

◊ ◊

Lincoln went to his law office that October morning as usual, planning to lead his normal life whether he became President or not. His office was as carelessly kept as his clothing. On top of his cluttered desk was a bundle of papers, new and old, on which Lincoln had scribbled a note: "When you can't find it anywhere else, look into this."

Old Abe found a surprise in his mail this morning.

There was a letter in the handwriting of a child, a young girl who lived near Lake Erie in Westfield, New York.

Her name was Grace Bedell.

Lincoln smiled as he read. Grace explained that her father had returned from a fair with a poster showing Lincoln and Hannibal Hamlin, who was running for Vice President:

Gorsline

Oct. 15, 1860

Hon. A B Lincoln,
Dear Sir

   ... I am a little girl only eleven years old, but want you should be President of the United States very much so I hope you won't think me very bold to write to such a great man as you are. Have you any little girls about as large as I am if so give them my love and tell her to write to me if you cannot answer this letter. I have got 4 brother's and part of them will vote for you anyway and if you will let your whiskers grow I will try and get the rest of them to vote for you   you would look a great deal better for your face is so thin. All the ladies like whiskers and they would tease their husbands to vote for you and then you would be President. My father is a going to vote for you and if I was a man I would vote for you to but I will try and get every one to vote for you that I can. ...

   I must not write any more   answer this letter right off.

Good bye
Grace Bedell

Mr. Lincoln did not know it, of course, but Grace Bedell had learned a great deal about him from her father, who had read of Lincoln's life in newspapers. Grace especially liked stories of Lincoln's boyhood, and often thought of him lying on the floor of a log cabin in the wilderness, studying his lessons by the light of a roaring fire.

"If only I could study like that," Grace thought, "there's no telling how famous I might become."

The blue-eyed, brown-haired little girl lived with her parents and her brothers and sisters in a white frame house on Washington Street in Westfield. Though she was small for her age, Grace had a lively mind and sometimes talked more like a grown-up than a child.

The day Mr. Bedell brought home a Republican poster and showed it to his children, Grace was dismayed. She stared at the badly printed pictures of Mr. Lincoln and Hannibal Hamlin. Then she shook her head over Lincoln.

"He looks so thin," she thought. "I'm just going to write and tell him so."

Without a word to her family, Grace went up to her room and carefully wrote a letter, the longest she had ever written. Grace could not keep her secret for long. A day or so after she mailed the letter she told her older sister about it. Her sister stared. "How on earth did you know how to address a famous man like Mr. Lincoln?"

"I'll show you," Grace said, and wrote the address she had put on her letter: "The Honorable A B Lincoln, Esquire." The whole Bedell family laughed over this, but Mrs. Bedell told the blushing Grace, "Well, that's one letter he'll be sure to get anyway. There's no doubt who it's meant for."

Mrs. Bedell was right. Lincoln not only received the letter promptly, but was so pleased with it that he wrote to Grace at once:

Miss Grace Bedell   *Springfield, Ills.*
                                        Oct. 19. 1860

My dear little Miss.
    Your very agreeable letter of the 15th, is received.

He explained that he had no little girl, but only three sons, aged seventeen, nine, and seven.

Then he wrote:

As to the whiskers, having never worn any, do you not think people would call it . . . silly . . . if I were to begin it now?

Your very sincere well-wisher.
A. Lincoln

Lincoln then turned to the piles of other letters and papers on his desk, and shook hands with many strangers who had come to wish him well or ask for jobs in Washington. He spent most of his time these days talking with men who were helping him in his race for President.

Among the crowd were many men who asked Lincoln to find jobs for them in Washington. Old Abe didn't refuse, but told one of these men a fable.

"Once," he said, "a King was out hunting with the men of his court and met a farmer. 'It's going to rain,' the farmer said.

"The King turned to his magician, who shook his head and said it would not rain. About an hour later the hunting party was soaked by a rainstorm.

"The King cut off the magician's head and sent for the farmer and offered him the job.

" 'It ain't me that knows when it's going to rain,' the farmer said, 'it's my jackass. He lays his ears back.'

"The King appointed the jackass the court magician. But he soon realized it was the biggest mistake of his life—because every jackass in the country wanted a job."

Sometimes Lincoln met with important visitors in his home. One night when he was talking with several political leaders, his young son Tad entered and called in a loud whisper, "Ma says come to supper."

Lincoln smiled and turned to his guests. "You've all heard, gentlemen, the announcement about the state of affairs in the dining room. If I'm elected, it will never do to make this young man a member of my cabinet; it's plain he can't be trusted with the secrets of state."

But somehow, no matter how busy he was that day, Lincoln could not forget Grace Bedell and her letter.

Mr. Lincoln rubbed his smooth chin and smiled. It was an odd idea to think of himself in whiskers. In this year of 1860, beards were not fashionable in America and there were few whiskered faces to be seen. But of course Mr. Lincoln cared nothing for fashion. The more he thought of it the more he thought he would grow a beard and see if he might look more like a President.

Perhaps he thought his face would not look so long and bony. Perhaps he thought he would not be quite so ugly with a beard.

Whatever he thought, Old Abe decided to try Grace Bedell's idea.

One morning soon afterward he went to his office without shaving. A day or so later, people began to notice a dark stubble along his jaws. Grace's wish was beginning to come true.

The people of the country voted for a new President on
November 6. Even on that day Mr. Lincoln went to his office, where hundreds of friends and well-wishers crowded in
to see him. Someone suggested that he close the doors to keep
them out. "No," Mr. Lincoln said. "I've never closed doors
on my friends and I don't intend to start now."

"Let's go and vote, Abe," said a friend.

"I'm not going to vote."

"What!"

"No," Lincoln said. "I just can't vote for myself, and I
surely won't vote for a Democrat who supports slavery."

"Oh, I'll fix that." When they reached the polling place his friend cut Lincoln's name from the top of a ballot so that Old Abe could vote for the other Republicans who were running for office.

After he had voted, Lincoln went to the telegraph office to wait for election news from other parts of the country, for there were no telephones, radios, or television sets. It was a long wait. After midnight the news began to come in over the telegraph wires. Pennsylvania had voted for Lincoln. New York, too. Then Maine, New Hampshire, and Ohio. Seventeen states in all. Abraham Lincoln had been elected as the sixteenth President of the United States.

He went home to take the good news to Mrs. Lincoln—but that was not so easy.

Old Abe remembered that evening for a long time:

"I went to my bedroom and found my wife fast asleep. I gently touched her shoulder and said, 'Mary'; she made no answer. I spoke again, a little louder, saying, 'Mary, Mary, we are elected.' "

But Mary Lincoln was a sound sleeper and her husband was too thoughtful to shake her awake or shout in her ear. "Well," Lincoln recalled, "I then went to bed. . . ."

And so Mrs. Lincoln had to wait until the next morning to learn that her dream had come true and that she was going to the White House at last.

Six weeks after Mr. Lincoln was elected, the state of South Carolina withdrew from the Union. Five other Southern states joined her and formed the Confederate States of America. The divided nation was moving toward war.

In many parts of the South rebels made plans to take over United States forts and Navy yards, arsenals and mints.

Southern soldiers fired cannon at a United States ship carrying supplies to Fort Sumter in the harbor of Charleston,

South Carolina. The South was ready to begin a civil war that was to take the lives of half a million Americans.

By now Old Abe's beard was attracting public attention. On December 27 the Evansville, Indiana, *Daily Journal* became the first newspaper to take note of it, by reporting that the President-elect had begun raising "a pair of whiskers," as if that were as important as the breaking up of the Union.

Meanwhile, Lincoln prepared to take over the presidency and try to keep the country from falling apart. He announced that he would go to Washington by train, traveling across the Middle West and the North for twelve days, stopping in as many cities as he could.

Friends begged Lincoln to travel to the capital in secrecy so that he would meet no crowds—or even take his oath of office in his home, so that no angry Southerners might harm him. When one of his close friends told Lincoln he might not live to be inaugurated, Old Abe only laughed.

Lincoln's mail was now filled with threats and warnings that he would be killed before he took office as President. People from many states, North and South, sent funeral wreaths, pictures of coffins, and skulls and crossbones. Lincoln refused to worry. All would turn out well, he insisted.

He did not fear crowds. He wanted to give the people a chance to see their new President, beard and all, and to tell them how he felt about saving the Union. The chief reason for the trip was to calm the people's fears that war was coming because he had been elected. He hoped to convince them that the North and the South could continue to live together in peace.

And so, on the morning of February 11, 1861, Mr. Lincoln left Springfield for the last time in his life. Most of the town's nine thousand people crowded about the train station in a cold rain to see him off.

His new beard was now fairly well grown. Just two days before, he had sat for a photographer, the last picture made before he left home, and the first showing the bewhiskered Lincoln—it was this picture which was to appear long afterward on the United States five-dollar bill. Strangely enough Mr. Lincoln made no mention of his family's remarks about his beard. If his wife liked it, she never said so. His friends certainly teased him about it at first, but Old Abe's good-humored replies were not written down.

Lincoln said good-bye to his wife and two younger sons, who were to join him in Indianapolis that night, and then went aboard the crowded little train. His older son, Robert, and many friends from Illinois went with him. Lincoln had been warned to carry dozens of guards with him, but he refused. "No," he said, "I want to see the people, and to be seen by them. I'm not afraid. I won't be treated like a prisoner of war. I'm public property now and the public has a right to inspect me." Mr. Lincoln had his way. Only four army officers went aboard as guards.

Lincoln made a short speech from the rear of the train. He removed his tall hat and raised his arm above the crowd, then gripped the railing and said, "My dear friends . . . No one, not in my situation, can appreciate my feelings of sadness at this parting. To this place, and to the kindness of you people, I owe everything. I have lived here a quarter of a century, and passed from a young to an old man. Here my children have been born and one is buried. I now leave, not knowing when or whether ever I may return. . . . I bid you an affectionate farewell."

No one could know that Mr. Lincoln would never see Springfield again.

The little train then moved away, puffing steam and black woodsmoke. Behind the engine was its tender, piled

high with firewood. And behind that only two cars, one for baggage and one for passengers. Both cars were painted bright yellow.

The train rolled through the Illinois countryside, halting at many small towns. There was one stop at the village of State Line, on the Indiana border, where there was a change of locomotives. Lincoln and his friends ate in the station, poor food "at double the regular price," as a newspaper reporter said. Then Lincoln said a few words to a crowd that had gathered, people in wagons, buggies, and carriages, and on horseback; some in buckskins and coonskin caps, others in the fashionable dress of the day, with fine beaver hats on their heads. These people were anxious to see the first President born west of the Appalachian Mountains. Everyone wanted to get a look at the "Rail-Splitter" of whom they knew so little.

The Republicans had tried to tell his life story to the people of the country, but Lincoln was too modest to be of much

help. "There's so little of me to tell," he said. But in each town, when he saw the crowds about the train, Lincoln felt himself at home. In one town he began one of his tales.

"I'll tell a story, if you'll promise not to let it out.

"Once I knew a man who was running for sheriff, who owned a horse that he was mighty proud of. The horse was slow and stubborn, but surefooted and a good worker. My friend rode about the county on this horse, trying to get votes.

"On the morning of the election he mounted his old horse to go to the courthouse. His horse lagged, and stopped to bite at every bush and twig—"

At that moment the locomotive puffed loudly and pulled away, cutting the story in half. Lincoln waved and the crowd yelled to him, "We'll never let out *that* story!"

A few miles beyond, the train stopped in the town of Lebanon, Indiana, where Lincoln saw people running down the tracks toward him.

One of Lincoln's friends laughed, and joked, "Here come the folks from that last town to hear the rest of your story."

Lincoln told the Lebanon crowd what had happened at his last stop and then told the rest of the story.

"The lagging horse, stopping to bite at every juicy sprig, was so slow the candidate was too late arriving at the court-house, couldn't enter his nomination, and lost out." The crowd laughed and Lincoln waved as the train moved on once more. "Farewell. I can't afford to miss the inauguration—and if my journey goes on at this rate it'll be resurrection day be-fore I reach the capital."

At the end of the day the train reached Indianapolis, where the bands played and cannon were fired in Lincoln's honor and a parade led the way to a hotel where he spent the night. Lincoln made another speech to about twenty thou-sand people who had been waiting in the street to hear him, and then tried to shake hands with everyone who squeezed into the hotel to greet him. He stood the pushing and shoving until he had shaken so many hands that his arm hurt, and then retreated to his rooms. "That's harder work than split-ting rails," he said.

Mrs. Lincoln and the younger boys, Tad and Willie, joined Lincoln in the city, and some of Old Abe's friends went back home, making room on the train for the Lincoln family.

Day after day the train went from town to town, with so many stops that Mr. Lincoln grew hoarse from making speeches.

At one stop a crowd called for Mrs. Lincoln, and Old Abe went into the train and brought her out. The people saw a pretty, blue-eyed, brown-haired woman who was plump and not very tall.

Mr. Lincoln put his arm around his wife and said, "Here

Gorsline

we are—I'm giving you the long and short of it." The crowd laughed and cheered as the train pulled off.

On some days he was kept so busy that he had no time for meals. Each night he stopped in a large city, where he rode in a shining carriage behind six horses with plumes on their heads and flags in their harnesses. He rode along streets hung with red, white, and blue banners and roaring with the cheers of great crowds. Though he was very tired, he waved and shook hands and made still more speeches.

He told the people he would do his best to save the Union. He said that the President himself was not important, but that the country was great, and would be great for many years to come. If he was not a good President, Mr. Lincoln said, the people could send him back to Springfield and try another man.

Lincoln's train moved on to Cincinnati and Columbus, Ohio, then to Pittsburgh, Pennsylvania, and back again into Ohio, turning north toward Cleveland.

At a small town in Pennsylvania a big coal miner called from the crowd.

"Abe, they say you're the tallest man in the United States, but I don't believe you're any taller than I am."

"Come up here and let's measure," Lincoln said.

The dusty miner in his work clothes shouldered through the crowd, climbed on the train, and stood back to back with Lincoln.

An army officer came up and felt the two heads with his hand.

"They're exactly the same height," he said. The crowd cheered and the two tall men shook hands.

A man in an Ohio town handed Lincoln a whistle made from a pig's tail. He blew into it until his cheeks puffed and the new whiskers stood out straight, like porcupine quills. The whistle made a loud screech. Lincoln laughed. "I never thought there was music in such a thing as that."

At one stop Tad and Willie Lincoln played leapfrog in a hotel lobby, and their father made one or two leaps with them, flying through the air with his long, thin legs, just to show that he could keep up with them. Tad and Willie often played jokes on people who crowded about their father. Their favorite trick was to whisper to someone, "Do you want to see Old Abe?" and then point out some stranger in the crowd and hide to watch the confusion.

At one railroad station Lincoln's voice failed and he could not make a speech. He waved to the crowd and smiled and stroked his new beard. A man stepped up and handed him two shiny red apples. A small boy tried to warn the new President that the man expected a favor in return. "Say, Mr.

Lincoln," he yelled, "that man is running for postmaster." Lincoln laughed with the crowd as the train pulled away.

The train, now pulled by a new engine named the *Rocket*, passed through Erie, Pennsylvania, and along the shore of Lake Erie. Soon it entered New York State.

When Lincoln learned that the train was soon to stop in Westfield, he thought of his young friend Grace, and told men on the train about her letter. "It was so different from all the others that it was a relief and a pleasure, so I answered it right away. I hope I can see that little girl."

In the tall white house where her family lived on Washington Street, Grace Bedell had spent the day preparing for Lincoln's arrival. Since she did not know when his train would reach the town, she put on her best dress and coat about noon. Then with her two sisters and a young man from the neighborhood, she joined the rest of the people of Westfield at the depot.

She was unnoticed in the excited, bustling crowd. Grace carried a bunch of red roses for Mr. Lincoln, the gift of a friend who had a greenhouse in her backyard. Holding the flowers carefully, she stood with her sisters and the neighbor in the rear of the crowd and waited. Time dragged slowly, but at last, near two P.M., there was a piercing whistle and the little train rolled into sight.

The engine halted at the depot in clouds of steam and black smoke. Men ran about to get wood and water for the engine. Lincoln appeared at the rear of the train and waved to the cheering crowd.

"I can't make a speech for two reasons," he said. "First, I'm so hoarse that I can scarcely make a sound. Second, I have no speech to make, and if I had, it would hardly be proper to make it."

The croaking voice halted and Lincoln looked about, smiling, "Seeing the large crowd of people, I came out to look at you, and I suppose you came here to look at me. And from the large number of ladies I see in the crowd, I think I have much the best of the bargain." The crowd laughed.

Of all this Grace Bedell knew nothing. She was so small that she could not see Lincoln for the crowd, and did not hear his voice over the noise about the depot.

Gripping her bouquet of roses tightly, Grace began to blink back tears. Mr. Lincoln had forgotten. She was not going to see him after all.

Lincoln cleared his throat and called to the people nearest the train.

"I had a letter from a little girl in this place, and if she is here I would like to meet her."

The crowd was still.

"Who is it?" someone asked. "Tell us her name."

"Her name is Grace Bedell. Is Grace here?"

There was a stir beside the tracks as the Bedell girl's companion, Mr. McCormack, took Grace by the hand and led her through the crowd to a low platform beside the train. People stood on their toes and craned their necks to get a better view.

"She wrote me that she thought I would be better looking if I wore whiskers," Lincoln said.

Then he stepped down from his car, shook the flustered girl's hand, and kissed her.

"You see," he said, "I let these whiskers grow for you, Grace." The crowd cheered.

Grace hardly noticed his whiskers, and did not stop to notice whether Mr. Lincoln's face was less homely now. She thought only, "How kind he looks. And how sad."

The surprise of Lincoln's kiss and the staring crowd were

too much for Grace. No sooner had his hand moved from her
shoulder than she darted for home. Grace ran. She stopped
for nothing, spoke to no one, and looked at no one.

She dodged in and out between horses and buggies, around carriages waiting in the street, and even crawled under a wagon blocking her way. She raced for home as fast as her little legs could carry her.

When she stood at the front door of her home, panting, she saw for the first time that she had forgotten to give Mr. Lincoln his flowers. She still clutched in her hand the stems of the roses. Soon her brothers came home, too, and teased her about the forgotten flowers—perhaps because they were jealous of the attention Mr. Lincoln had given Grace.

Back at the depot, the train puffed and began to creep off toward Buffalo, with a wail of its whistle. The tall figure of Mr. Lincoln grew smaller and smaller. The people of Westfield watched until he was out of sight. Few of them would ever see him again, but none would forget him.

The story of Grace and Mr. Lincoln and his beard was told in many newspapers across the country:

Old Abe Kissed by Pretty Girl.

Whiskers Win Winsome Miss.

Artists and photographers made pictures of Lincoln with the new beard.

People in other towns where the train stopped began to notice that Lincoln seemed younger and better looking than they had expected from stories in the newspapers.

One woman who had traveled a long distance to see Mr. Lincoln took a good look at him and said, "I knew it was a lie. I just knew it was."

One of Old Abe's friends turned to her. "What do you mean, Madam?"

"When I left home my neighbors told me I'd find Mr.

Lincoln was very ugly. It was all a lie. He's the handsomest man I ever saw in my life."

Even people who found Lincoln homely felt better about the new President when they saw his kindly face. Perhaps this was because Mrs. Lincoln took such good care of him, as she did when their train pulled into New York City. Mrs. Lincoln looked out at the waiting crowd and pulled a comb from her handbag. "Abraham," she said, "I must fix you up a little for these city folks." And she combed out his stiff hair and the bristly new beard until she was satisfied. Everyone seemed to agree that the beard made Abraham Lincoln a new man. And so it did.

From that time onward Americans forgot that Abraham Lincoln had ever been seen with deep hollows in his cheeks and his long sharp chin smooth and bare. For more than a hundred years afterward Americans were to see Mr. Lincoln's bearded face on their coins and stamps, in paintings and photographs, and on statues. The beard became so familiar and natural a part of Lincoln's appearance that Americans could no more think of him without it than they could imagine a clean-shaven Santa Claus.

When Lincoln went on from Westfield to Washington and became President, he went as a bearded Father Abraham, as the people of his day sometimes called him. Lincoln was to lead the nation through the horrors of the Civil War and free the slaves. He was also to die from the bullet of an assassin a week after Federal troops had triumphed and the United States were united once more, for the first time a land where all were free.

Mr. Lincoln was the first American president to wear a beard—but he set such a lasting fashion that of the next nine Presidents who were to serve after him only one was clean-shaven.

Mr. Lincoln's face, the long face that was to become one of the most famous faces in history, had been changed forever. All because of Grace Bedell.

Gorsline

Author's Note

Though historians have often mentioned Mr. Lincoln's beard and his correspondence with Grace Bedell, they have had little to say about the girl who suggested the most famous whiskers in American history.

Grace's own story of meeting Lincoln appeared in a Westfield, New York, newspaper in 1930, and her letter, which had been saved by the Lincoln family, was reproduced in a Detroit newspaper soon afterward. In her later life Grace often told her three grandchildren of the incident.

A Westfield man who was in the crowd when Lincoln met Grace in 1861 also described the scene in his diary. Until now, these accounts have not found their way into books.

Grace returned with her parents to her birthplace in Albion, New York, soon after her meeting with Lincoln. There she entered the Albion Academy where she met a young teacher, George H. Billings, a former Union army sergeant.

Grace and George were married in 1867 and later moved to Kansas, where they reared their only child, Harlow, on their farm homestead. Later George became president of a bank in Delphos, Kansas, which is still chiefly owned by his three grandsons.

Grace Bedell Billings died in Kansas on November 2, 1936, two days before her 88th birthday.

The letter from Lincoln, her most prized possession, was later sold by the grandsons (George, Arthur, and Roger Billings) to settle the family estate. By then the letter, yellow with age, was beginning to deteriorate, and it was felt that it should be in the hands of experts who could preserve it.

The letter has been sold twice over the years. In 1977 a Dallas merchant offered it for sale as "one of Lincoln's most famous letters." The price was $67,000.

To young readers of this story about Grace Bedell and Abraham Lincoln I can only repeat what Mr. Lincoln once said when he was asked to comment on a book: "For those who like this kind of a book, this is the kind of book they will like."

Burke Davis
Williamsburg, Va.

The letters exchanged by Grace Bedell and Mr. Lincoln have been shortened for use in this book, so that they may be more easily understood.

Gorsline

Because of their importance, the complete correspondence appears on the following pages.

Oct. 15, 1860

Hon A B Lincoln
Dear Sir

My father has just (come) home from the fair and brought home your picture and Mr. Hamlin's. I am a little girl only eleven years old, but want you should be President of the United States very much so I hope you wont think me very bold to write such a great man as you are. Have you any little girls about as large as I am if so give them my love and tell her to write to me if you cannot answer this letter. I have got 4 brother's and part of them will vote for you anyway and if you will let your whiskers grow I will try and get the rest of them to vote for you you would look a great deal better for your face is so thin. All the ladies like whiskers and they would tease their husband's to vote for you and then you would be President. My father is going to vote for you and if I was a man I would vote for you to but I will try and get every one to vote for you that I can. I think that rail fence around your picture makes it look very pretty I have got a little baby sister she is nine weeks old and just as cunning as can be. When you direct your letter dir(e)ct to Grace Bedell Westfield Chataque County New York

I must not write any more   answer this letter right off

Good bye
Grace Bedell

Miss. Grace Bedell   *Springfield, Ills.*
                                         Oct 19. 1860

My dear little Miss.
    Your very agreeable letter of the 15th, is received.
    I regret the necessity of saying I have no daughters.
I have three sons—one seventeen, one nine, and one seven,
years of age. They, with their mother, constitute my whole
family.
    As to the whiskers, having never worn any, do you
not think people would call it a piece of silly affection if
I were to begin it now?
                        Your very sincere well-wisher
                        A. Lincoln

About the author

Burke Davis is a native of North Carolina, where he attended Duke University, Guilford College, and the University of North Carolina. He worked for several years on newspapers in North Carolina and Maryland before joining the staff of the Colonial Williamsburg Restoration.

Mr. Davis is the author of more than thirty books for both adults and young readers, including *To Appomattox: Our Incredible Civil War*. His most recent book for Coward, McCann & Geoghegan was *Runaway Balloon: The Last Flight of Confederate Air Force One*.

Mr. Davis and his wife, Evangeline, make their home in Williamsburg, Virginia.

About the artist

Douglas Gorsline has illustrated many books for children and is perhaps best known for his depictions of American historical subjects. Among his previous books are *The Vicksburg Veteran*, *Me and Willie and Pa*, and *Gettysburg: Tad Lincoln's Story*, all by F. N. Monjo. This is his first book for Coward, McCann & Geoghegan.

Mr. Gorsline grew up in New York State. For a number of years he has lived in the Burgundy region of France.